AMERICAN LEGENDS™

Johnny Appleseed

Marianne Johnston

The Rosen Publishing Group's
PowerKids Press™
New York

JB10
APPLESEED

Published in 2001 by The Rosen Publishing Group, Inc.
29 East 21st Street, New York, NY 10010

First Edition

Book Design: Michael de Guzman

Photo Credits: pp. 4, 16, 19 © North Wind Pictures; p. 7 © Skjold Photographs; p. 8 © State of Ohio Department of Industrial and Economic Development/FPG International; p. 11 © 1994 North Wind Pictures; p. 15 CORBIS/Bettmann; p. 20 by MaryJane Wojciechowski.

Johnston, Marianne.
    Johnny Appleseed / by Marianne Johnston.
        p. cm.— (American legends)
    Includes index.
    Summary: Describes the life and the legend of the frontiersman known as Johnny Appleseed.
    ISBN 0-8239-5577-X (lib. bdg. : alk. paper)
    1. Appleseed, Johnny, 1774–1845—Juvenile literature. 2. Apple growers—United States—Biography—Juvenile literature.
3. Frontier and pioneer life—Middle West—Juvenile literature. [1. Appleseed, Johnny, 1774–1845. 2. Apple growers.
3. Frontier and pioneer life.] I. Title. II. American legends (New York, N.Y.)

SB63.C46 J65 2000
634'.11'092—dc21
[B]   99-088260

Manufactured in the United States of America

18.75 RL 10/01

Contents

The legend of Johnny Appleseed says he carried a bag full of apple seeds and looked for fertile, or rich, land in which to plant them. He planted his first orchard next to the Brokenstraw River in Pennsylvania, just south of a town called Warren. The year was 1797.

Johnny Appleseed

A man wearing a tin pot for a hat **roamed** the green hills and rich valleys of Ohio, Indiana, and Pennsylvania. He carried a bag full of apple seeds on his back.

He looked for good places to plant apple seeds. Places by **creeks** or in meadows were best. This man who planted seeds was called Johnny Appleseed. He is an American **legend**.

What Is a Legend?

Many people around the world honor legends. A legend is a story that has come down from the past. We make heroes out of people who have qualities that we admire. In the case of Johnny Appleseed, gentleness, bravery, and kindness to others are the qualities we admire and would like to have ourselves.

Stories are often told about our heroes. With each telling, the stories may grow more unreal. The **exaggeration** makes them charming and fun. The stories help people remember the special qualities of the **legendary** person. Sometimes the person is given a nickname, or a funny and interesting name. This nickname usually has something to do with a fact tied to that person. Johnny Appleseed is a good example.

People enjoy reading about legends, or stories that come down to us from the past. Such stories are not always about actual events from the past. Sometimes they go beyond the truth. This means that parts of the legends may have been made up.

Many monuments, such as this one in Ohio, have been built to remember Johnny Appleseed. His planting of apple trees across the American wilderness helped many hungry families on the frontier.

Who Was Johnny Appleseed?

Johnny Appleseed's real name was John Chapman. He was born in Leominster, Massachusetts, on September 26, 1774.

Before he turned two years old, Johnny's mom died. His father remarried when Johnny was almost six years old. As Johnny grew older, the Chapman house became full of children.

As a boy, Johnny loved to explore the woods near his home. He learned to love nature. Johnny's thirst for adventure grew as he got older. At the age of 23, Johnny left Massachusetts and set out for the western **frontier**.

Frontier Life and Times

The United States slowly became a country. **Settlers** from the east began to move west to live. They took land from Native Americans who were already living there. In the 1790s, settlers had only come as far as Ohio and Indiana. This land was called the western frontier.

Johnny's mission was to plant as many apple seeds as he could so that the settlers would have some food to eat. The lives of **pioneers** were very hard. Settlers had to clear land to set up farms. They also had to build houses for shelter. Johnny's seeds grew into trees that helped the pioneers get started with their farms. If a family was too poor to buy an apple tree, he would give it to the family for free.

Pioneers on the frontier had to clear a patch of land to set up their homes. Often, settlers were very poor. The apples from Johnny's trees were the perfect food for them. Settlers could make cider to drink and sauces and apple butter to eat.

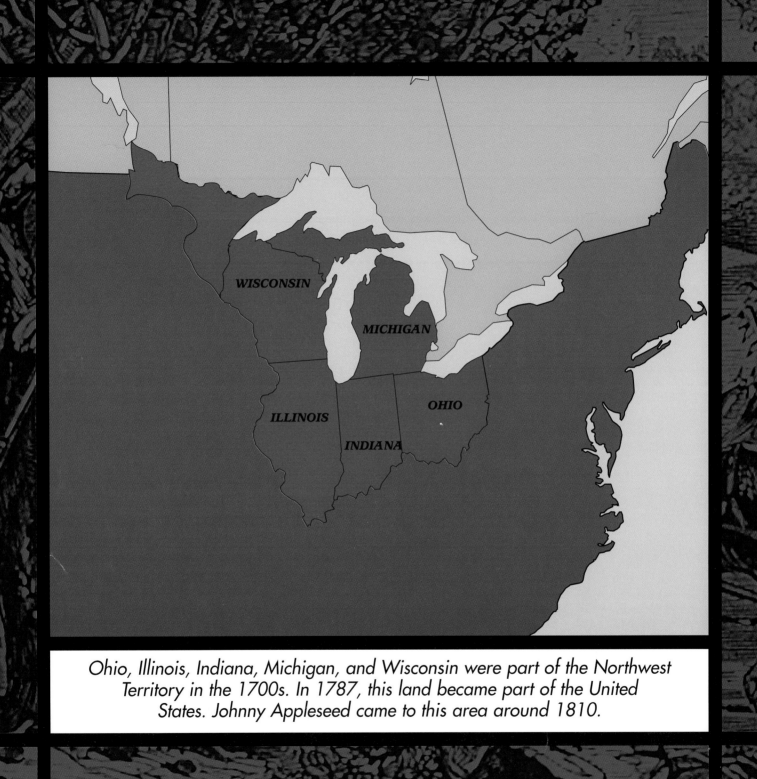

WISCONSIN

MICHIGAN

ILLINOIS

OHIO

INDIANA

Ohio, Illinois, Indiana, Michigan, and Wisconsin were part of the Northwest Territory in the 1700s. In 1787, this land became part of the United States. Johnny Appleseed came to this area around 1810.

Johnny and His Orchards

Johnny made his way to northwestern Pennsylvania after he left Massachusetts in 1797. He spent a few years in Pennsylvania, planting his first **orchards**. In the early 1800s, he journeyed on, moving into the **Northwest Territory**. Johnny planted his apple seeds and then waited for settlers to arrive. He sold the young trees to the settlers when they came to live in the area. The trees could be **transplanted**, or moved, to the settlers' homes.

Johnny's **supply** of apple seeds came from Pennsylvania. People at the cider mills threw the apple seeds away. He gathered them from the cider mills. Johnny walked great distances with his sacks of seeds. He walked barefoot most of the time.

A Strange-Looking Person

People stopped and stared at Johnny Appleseed wherever he traveled. Many people thought he looked strange because of the way he dressed. According to legend, or stories from the past, he was a thin man. He had long, black hair. He wore shirts made from old cotton sacks. These sacks had been used to carry coffee. Johnny cut holes in the tops and sides of the sacks for his head and arms. He wore torn pants, sometimes four or five pairs at once.

Johnny went barefoot for most of the year. When he did wear shoes, they were usually mismatched. Sometimes they did not fit. Sometimes only one of his feet had a shoe on it! If these stories are true, Johnny Appleseed was indeed a strange-looking person.

Many people thought Johnny looked strange because of what he wore. It is said that he wore a tin pot on his head for a hat. At suppertime he would use the pot to cook his dinner over a campfire. Then he would clean it and use it as a hat again.

Many frontier families knew Johnny. Whenever he visited families, he loved to bring presents and tell stories to the children. When he stayed overnight with families, he would sleep on the floor. He didn't need a bed. Johnny liked to keep his life simple.

A Kind and Gentle Man

Frontier settlers who knew Johnny Appleseed said he was one of the kindest and gentlest people they had ever known. When he visited frontier families, he would bring colored ribbons as presents for the little girls of the household. He loved to tell stories to the boys and girls he visited.

Johnny also became friends with the Native Americans he met. In the early 1800s, many settlers were afraid of the Native Americans. Many Native Americans were angry that the settlers had taken their land. Johnny Appleseed treated them with kindness, though, and he got kindness in return.

The Fearless Planter of Seeds

Johnny Appleseed was very brave. Bears, wolves, snakes, and wild pigs with big **tusks** roamed the forests in the early 1800s. Johnny was not scared to travel and sleep in the woods by himself. He never carried a gun for protection. He did not believe in killing or hunting animals.

Johnny's feet grew tough and strong because he walked barefoot. One cold winter's day in Pennsylvania, Johnny proved how tough his feet were. He walked for miles across the icy surface of a frozen lake without wearing any shoes! It is also said that Johnny Appleseed was so healthy that he never got sick until the end of his life.

Johnny Appleseed often traveled in the woods alone. He was not afraid, even though there were wolves, bears, and wild boars in the woods.

The legend of Johnny Appleseed tells about him traveling barefoot in the woods in winter. It is also said that he could sleep anywhere, even at the foot of a nearby tree.

Johnny Loved All Creatures

In the 1800s, many horses were let loose in the woods to die once they had become too old to work. Johnny felt sorry for these horses. He would round them up and find people to take care of them.

One cold, snowy night, after a long day of work, Johnny was ready to go to sleep. It is said that he crawled into a hollow log lying on the forest floor. Much to his surprise, he found a mother bear and her cubs snoozing inside the log! Johnny was not scared. He crept quietly out of the log and laid his head at the foot of a nearby tree. He did not even make a campfire on that cold night. He did not want to disturb the sleeping bears.

Remembering Johnny Appleseed

During the cold spring of 1845, Johnny was taking care of an apple orchard near Fort Wayne, Indiana. The freezing spring air was too hard on the 70-year-old Johnny. He came down with **pneumonia**. Johnny died a few days later on March 18, 1845, at a friend's cabin in Fort Wayne.

Today a **memorial** to Johnny Appleseed stands at Archer Park in Fort Wayne, Indiana. The words "He Lived for Others" are carved on a marker there. Each fall, the people of Fort Wayne hold a festival in his honor. Visitors come to learn what life was like for settlers in Johnny's time. Actors wear frontier costumes and show visitors how people lived as pioneers. Johnny Appleseed is truly an American legend.

Glossary

creeks (KREEKS) Small streams that flow from a river.

exaggeration (eckz-ah-jer-AY-shun) Something made to seem larger or more amazing than it really is.

frontier (frun-TEER) The edge of a settled country, where the wilderness begins.

legend (LEH-jend) A story passed down through the years that many people believe.

legendary (LEH-jend-ayr-ee) To be famous and important.

memorial (me-MOR-ee-al) Something built to remember a person.

Northwest Territory (north-WEST TEHR-uh-tohr-ee) An area of land located west of Pennsylvania. It became part of the United States in 1787.

orchards (OR-cherdz) Areas where fruit trees are grown.

pioneers (py-uh-NEERS) The first people to settle in a new area.

pneumonia (noo-MOHN-ya) A disease that people can get in their lungs.

roamed (ROHMD) When a person has traveled for a long way without an exact idea of where he or she would end up.

settlers (SEH-tuh-lers) People who move to a new land to live.

supply (suh-PLY) A large amount of an item that has been gathered and saved for use in the future.

transplanted (TRANZ-plant-ed) Something that has been moved from one place and has been put down in another.

tusks (TUSKS) Long, large pointed teeth that come out of the mouths of some animals.

Index

Web Sites

To learn more about Johnny Appleseed, check out these Web sites:
http://johnnyappleseedfest.com/
http://www.richnet.net/richland/govt/parks/japple.htm